Jobs and Their Tools Over Time

Sukie Demers

Series Editor • Mark Pearcy

Firefighters put out fires.
They help people.
Firefighters use water
to put out fires.

In the past, they used buckets of water.

Today, they use hoses and fire engines.

Doctors help people who are sick or hurt. Doctors help keep people well.

Doctors use **medicine** and tools.

In the past, they used simple tools.

Today, they use computers.

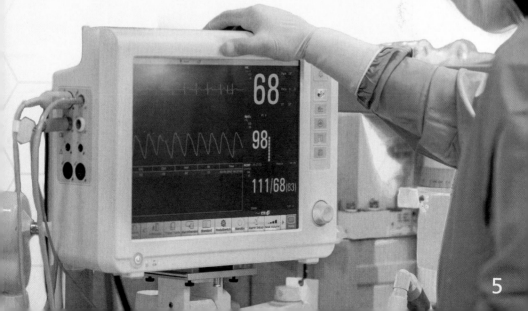

Farmers grow **crops** and raise animals. They produce food.

Farmers use machines.

In the past, they used animals to pull the machines.

Today, they use tractors to plow, plant, and harvest.

Teachers help people learn about the world.

In the past, they used books and chalk.

What tools do teachers use today?